Take a break

Dr. Lalit Mohan Gupta

"Life is not just about running, stop and think about what you want to do in life. Achieve your goal which you had made, but in the race of life you have lost it somewhere."

Dr. Lalit Mohan Gupta

"The important thing in life is to stop and think. Concentrate and you will find that there is something more important in your life than a job, that is to introduce yourself."

Dr. Lalit Mohan Gupta

How to read this book?

This book will help you to become a successful and intelligent person only if you apply the things written in this book in your daily life. In this book, some pages have been left blank for the readers, after completing any chapter, write your thoughts on that page and also write what you learned from that chapter. Life is the name of continuous learning, when you will read this book, there will be some stories at many places, which will touch your heart, the purpose of those stories is to make a place in the depths of your heart in reality so that you can learn from that chapter. To be able to store the related learning in his mind for a long time.

Do not try to understand by reading this book completely at once, it is like if a lion hunts an elephant at a time, it does not eat it whole at once, but in pieces Eats little by little, digests, then eats little by little in pieces, digests..... and this process goes on till he absorbs the full powers of the elephant in himself. That is until the lion makes himself strong by eating and digesting the flesh and flesh of the elephant. Similarly, readers are also requested to read this book little by little, read only one chapter in a day, and follow the lessons learned from it in life.

Index

Introduction

'Har Har Mahadev' Friends, with time there are many things that a person learns, time has also taught me many things, I am feeling very happy to share my life experience. You will find both bitter and sweet experiences of life in this book. First of all, I thank God, who gave me this opportunity to do this work in this life. To become successful in life, only hard work is not enough, but there is a need to work with full force in the right direction. I believe that to lead a good life, you should have good time management. Any management/organization/system should be designed to raise the standard of living and teach the art of living.

I will be happy to connect with you from my heart through this book, believe me, this book will bring a change in your life. You read the book till the end and try to mold it in life. Share happiness and say goodbye to troubles.

Many stories have been used by me while writing this book, believe me, a person is not able to remember facts or big things. But his nature is to remember stories and relate to them.

Stories compel our mind to imagine, it brings alive those persons in our mind.

I thank you from the bottom of my heart for choosing this book.

Gratitude

First of all thanks to God, who gave me such a lovely mother, whose love and blessings will remain indebted for life. My first mentor taught me to walk, speak, fight, and win.

Father is my second guru who taught me the art of living in society, in my defeat, in my victory, if anyone stood by me like a rock, it was my father. Father's powers are transmitted to me, whenever I lose, I remember my father's words, "Neither defeat is final, nor victory".

Heartfelt thanks to my brother who has helped me take many important decisions in life and thank my elder sister who is my elder sister as well as my good advisor.

I bow down and thank all my gurus, who have given me the light of knowledge, which gives me the ability to decide right and wrong in the dark paths.

In the end, I thank all my friends from the heart who taught me to live life freely and told me the value of friendship.

Chapter-1

Lose interest

Chapter-1

Lose interest

There comes a turning point in life when our enthusiasm starts running out. Our interest starts drifting away from almost everything in life. Our interest starts getting diverted even from friends, it seems as if our attachment has been lost from this world. This is something that is very frightening because in such a situation we do not feel like doing any work. This is the best situation when we should take a break in life and give time to ourselves. In the race of the world, people often get so busy working for others that they are unable to give time to themselves and when this happens, they become victims of depression. He starts kneeling inside. They feel that they have nothing to do in life, in such a situation, if you take some time away from everything, then it becomes easy for you to do something new. And when a person goes into a meditative state then he understands that this life is fleeting and it can end at some point. Then you start using your life to progress and do charity for others.

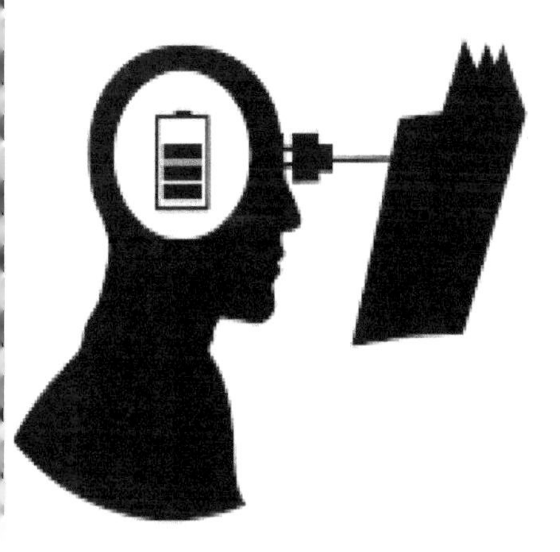

Summary & Lessons

The person who lives only and only for himself, in the end, finds misery. But the person who does something for others gets satisfaction. The most important thing in life is 'satisfaction'. This is not an easily attainable thing because human life is full of difficulties. So if you want to get satisfaction in life then take a break and focus on yourself.

What did you learn from this?

....

....

....

....

....

....

....

....

....

....

....

....

....

....

....

****

What change do you want in your life?

....

....

....

....

....

....

....

....

....

....

....

....

....

....

****

Chapter-2

Get angry quickly

Chapter-2

Get angry quickly

It is often seen that due to anger in their daily routine, a person commits many indecent actions. Because anger destroys a person's ability to think and creates a hindrance in their mental development. In such a situation, it is necessary to get rid of anger and calm the mind. In modern conditions, every person is a victim of this disease called anger. If anger is used wisely, it acts as an energy, at the initial level it is a simple emotion. When out of control, its consequences are dire. Anger is passion and passion damages relationships, self and mind. As a result, the person spoils the relationship with the people around him. Controlling anger is not easy, yet the person who is successful in controlling his anger is kept in the category of intelligent persons. The consequences of getting too angry are very bad. Often a person gets angry and starts abusing and misbehaving.

Usually, there is no need for a major reason for getting angry. Sometimes even the smallest things become a state of anger. It is believed that the main reason for getting angry is to be ambitious or not to talk about the mind. Anger affects the activities of daily living. Due to excessive anger, a person harms himself, his loved ones and the people working in his field of work. Anger always causes tension in relationships. In a state of anger, people lose their temper and start screaming.

Story

most dangerous weapon

When I was young, my father told a story that has a very deep meaning, I would like to share that story with you first.

One day we got tired while playing in the house, and told my mother to give me something to eat, 'I am very hungry, rats have created terror in my stomach'. Mother looked at him with love and said, wash your hands and face.

The comfort that a mother's sweet voice gives to the heart cannot be expressed with the lips. Well, when I went to wash my hands, I saw that the mother has brought a new glass vase to the house, now some new thing has come and the 'monkey inside me' should not jump, it cannot happen.

Due to my young age, low height as well as lack of complete control over my hands, I had to hold the vase in the hands that .... 'Dhadam' !! And then a voice came from inside what dropped. These children have created panic in the house. And then the mother appears in front of me, she got to see that fierce form in her eyes which she had not even imagined. Until some time ago, the mother who was talking with love in a sweet voice like honey, now the mother was looking like an incarnation of Mahakali. Then the mother gave one look at the broken vase and the other hand fell on the cheek faster than Bruce Lee's hands.

I was shocked, there is a special thing in Indian culture, mother loves a lot, but when she comes in front of us in another incarnation, then only God can save us.

After tasting Mother's hand, Mother scolded me a lot the hunger was completely gone. Exhausted, he went to the room and sat down. After a while, the mother abandoned the Mahakali avatar and the mother came in front of the incarnation of goddess Parvati then the same sweet way she started talking, son please eat food. Don't want to eat, I shouted and sat down in the bed. In such a situation, whatever efforts are made to persuade it, remains in vain. Mother also thought that he would agree after a while, but my stubbornness remained the same when it came to the evening.

No matter how angry a mother maybe, she cannot see her child hungry. Perhaps it is both his inner strength and weakness. This association starts in childhood, whenever the newborn cries, the mother pacifies him by breastfeeding. She naturally made up for it.

The evening began to fall, mother brought food many times and did all the efforts, but it is fun that someone should make me swoon.

It was time for dad to come when there was a knock at the door, he had just entered the house and seeing his face, he understood that something is wrong today. As is often the case, every husband understands 'what is the matter' just by looking into his wife's eyes. When he asked, Mataji said all the things that were on his tongue.

Now father came near and said what happened son. On hearing these words from my father, I broke down, my mother scolded and hit me today. I don't want to stay in this house I have to go to my grandparents, I will never come here again. Dad looked at me carefully and asked, tell me what happened. Now it was my turn to narrate the whole story, then father said: - Mother felt bad about this thing, I nodded my head, and said that in school there is even more severe beating. Dad smiled softly, I too could not stop my laughter. Meaning there is no abstinence from beating, then what is the point. I said scolding he felt bad.

On this father pointed to my mother and the plate of food was in front of me, father said to eat food and I will tell a story. Then father took a bite and put it in my mouth and said – let me tell you a story

Once upon a time, there was a king, there was prosperity in his kingdom but the king was very upset for some days, he wanted to know which is the most dangerous weapon?

He beat a trumpet to know that the king wanted that whoever would be presented with the 'most dangerous weapon' in front of the king, 'the one who inflicts the deepest wound', the king would reward with 1000 gold coins. Many people after hearing this news started bringing more than one weapon like a sword, spear, bow etc. But the king was that there was no name to be satisfied. Then a merchant son of the city heard this news from somewhere, he also reached the king's palace and bowed his head in front of the king. All the people were surprised that many Kshatriyas came and went and could not satisfy the king, so what weapon had he brought. Then the merchant's son raised a small box in front of the king, as soon as the king opened it, there was only a piece of paper in it. And seeing that some words were written on that piece of paper, the king began to think deeply for some time and after churning he said to the soldiers that this merchant son is appointed our minister, along with his hundred seals of gold. also, be provided.

Everyone was surprised that what was written on that piece of paper.

Do you know what was written on a piece of paper, it was written on it "Words of Wounds"

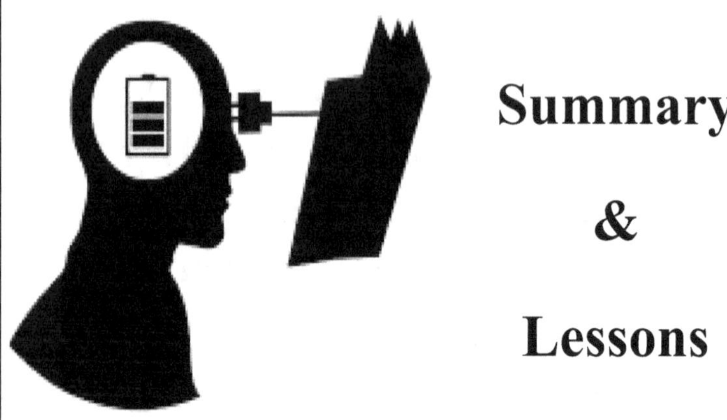

Summary & Lessons

Don't know how many lives have been ruined because of anger. A moment of anger can ruin your life, then you have no other way to take care of yourself and move on in life. The damage caused by anger can never be compensated. Yes, we can just push ourselves out of that situation. If a person wants that he should move ahead in life, then he should know how to handle the anger inside him. Getting angry is not a big deal, but controlling anger is a big deal.

What did you learn from this?

....

....

....

....

....

....

....

....

....

....

....

....

....

....

....

****

What change do you want in your life?

....

....

....

....

....

....

....

....

....

....

....

....

....

....

****

Chapter-3

Always tired

Chapter-3

Always tired

When you start feeling like you are always tired in life. So believe that you need to take a break in life. Sometimes a person becomes like a machine while working. His routine is such that he wakes up in the morning, gets ready, goes to the office, works, comes back in the evening, eats and goes to sleep and then repeats the same process the next day. If he does this for a few days, then it is understandable. But many of us

do not know how many people follow this routine for life and one day they leave the earth. If you always feel tired after work, then the reason behind this is your lack of interest in your work or your brain is tired of doing the same routine work.

Summary & Lessons

In such a situation, you need to take a break so that you can give time to yourself. I have also seen many such people who do not even take you even if they are given by the company, they do not even live, they need a machine throughout the year. If you keep working like that, then I have to say that friend, take out time for yourself, this life is found once, do something like that remember your name world

What did you learn from this?

....

....

....

....

....

....

....

....

....

....

....

....

....

....

....
****

What change do you want in your life?

....

....

....

....

....

....

....

....

....

....

....

....

....

....

****

Chapter-4

Feeling emotionally lost

Chapter-4

Feeling emotionally lost

Man is a creature made of emotions. In the workplace too, it is often seen that many times people are not able to control their emotions, any decision taken by the emotions can turn out to be a bad decision for the management in the future.

"Take control of your emotions and live your life,

or the people of this world will create turmoil in your life by throwing you in emotions".

Story

greatness comes from controlling emotions

Thomas Alva Edison, whom we know for his invention of the bulb, in reality, was different from any ordinary person in many ways. You can understand this after reading his life. I would like to share with you an incident from his life.

It is about the time when Edison was about 67 years old, his research and technology center was progressing very well. But one day God wanted to test them, believe that God passes all those great people once in life

through such terrible devastation which common man cannot tolerate, well let's move forward. Like I said that God takes the test, so maybe after seeing many successes in life, one day there was a fire in his factory, everything was burning in the fire. There everyone was standing and watching, some people were trying to put out the fire.

Just then, his young son, who was very worried, comes to him and sees the factory, which was burning in the fire. Then Edison's answer to his son was something like this, hearing which his son was stunned. Edison said 'Go get your mom and friends, they'll never see a fire like this again in life'

Such an answer can only be given by a great person in this situation, otherwise, an ordinary person may start complaining about losing everything.

Thomas Edison said that "the world has nothing for any man, but every man does something for the world."

Here the question arises whether his statements were just a hoax, then the answer would be no. Got out of tough situations.

Summary & Lessons

Emotions are an integral part of human life, when a child is born, he staggers and falls many times before learning to walk, at that time he does not have complete control over his feet, in the same way, emotions are inside man, but where and how And it takes a man a lot of time to learn why to use it, whether to do it or not.

Be it any battle of life without controlling your emotions, you will not be able to do even a small task well, says the battle.

You are a person working at any level of management if you do not know how to control your emotions and say anything anywhere and keep telling yourself that 'I am like this, or 'My heart' Whatever happens, I tell it 'So believe me, till now you have given unbearable pain to many people around you, which you cannot fix even if you want to.

Be wise, by getting control over your emotions, learn what to say, were to say, how to say or if the talk can hurt someone, then the best solution is "silence".

Never take any decision based on emotions.

Do not take any big decisions in these two situations, first when you are happy, second when you are sad.

What did you learn from this?

....

....

....

....

....

....

....

....

....

....

....

....

....

....

....

****

What change do you want in your life?

....

....

....

....

....

....

....

....

....

....

....

....

....

....

****

Chapter-5

Take things to heart

Chapter-5

Take things to heart

Some people take people's words to heart very quickly and such people are emotionally broken somewhere soon. This happens because the heart of these people is very innocent. These people never hurt others and because of doing so, people take advantage of their behaviour to hurt them and feel joy inside. If there is a person who takes things to

heart very quickly, then I believe that he has to face a lot of difficulties in life. This is because society is full of people who are engaged in hurting others. If you are the kind of person who quickly takes to heart what people say, then I believe that you should take a break in life and see if it is true. That is, how long will it last to take people's words to heart? How long will you keep harming yourself?

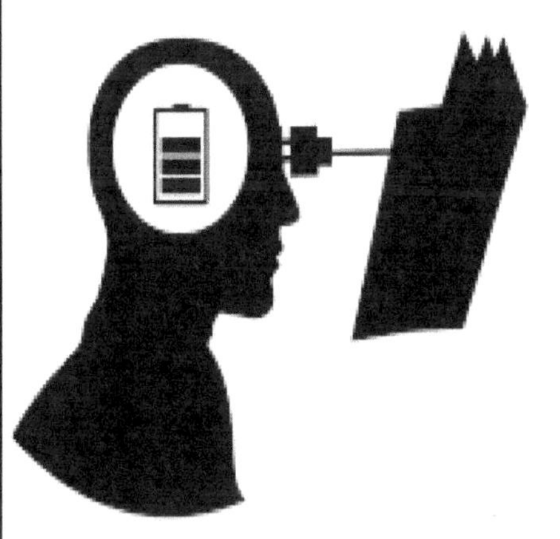

Summary & Lessons

The solution is to take a break in life and slowly try to understand that people will sometimes hurt you unknowingly or knowingly at times. But here it depends on how you behave or how you fight with that situation. You have to learn to fight this situation in your life otherwise people will keep on hurting you.

What did you learn from this?

……………………

………………………………………

………………………………………

………………………………………

………………………………………

………………………………………

……………………………………

………………………………………

………………………………………

………………………………………

………………………………………

………………………………………

………………………………………

………………………………………

………………………………………

****

What change do you want in your life?

....

....

....

....

....

....

....

....

....

....

....

....

....

....
****

Chapter-6

Overthinking

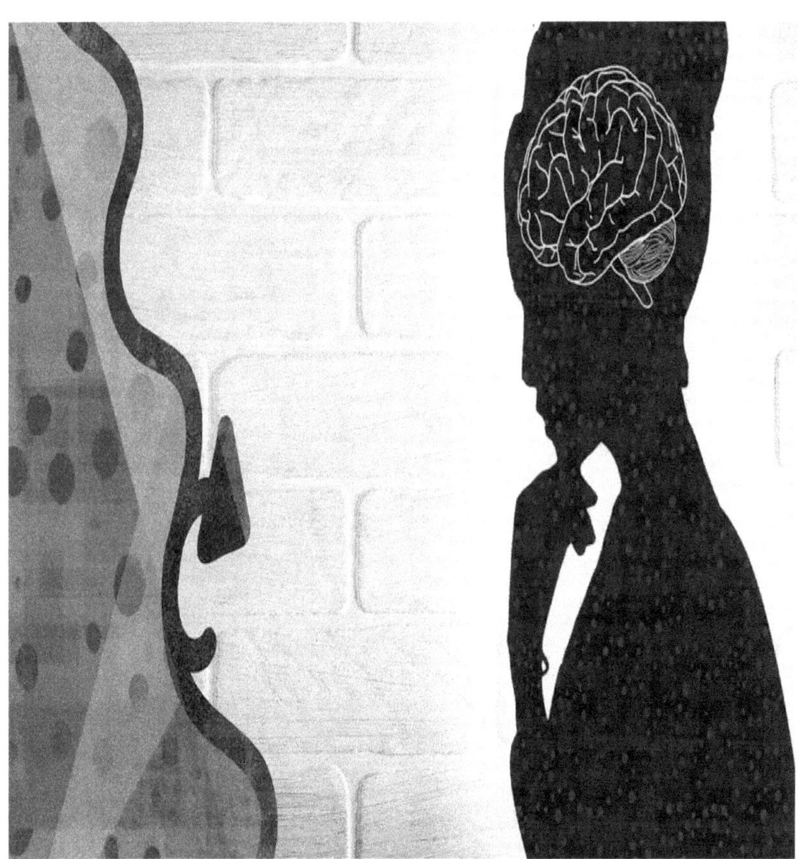

Chapter-6

Overthinking

Human is the only creature on earth, which has got the power to think so well. But if a person ruins himself because of his thinking power, then I believe that he should take a break in life. Many times I have seen some people who start thinking so much about small things that they start hurting themselves. People who think excessively forget in reality that thinking excessively becomes a cause of worry.

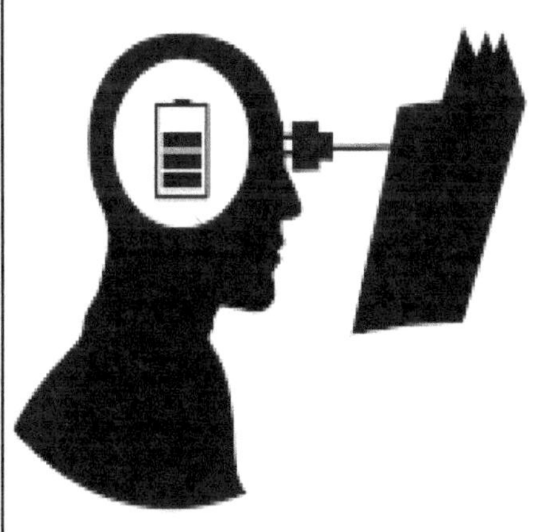

Summary & Lessons

I believe that there is a big difference between churning and thinking excessively and becoming anxious. be able to do better than If you are also included in this type of people, then I believe that stop thinking about others for a while and move ahead in life by using the powers of your mind.

What did you learn from this?

....

....

....

....

....

....

....

....

....

....

....

....

....

....

....

****

What change do you want in your life?

……………………

………………………………………

………………………………………

………………………………………

………………………………………

………………………………………

………………………………………

………………………………………

………………………………………

………………………………………

………………………………………

………………………………………

………………………………………

………………………………………

****

www.ingramcontent.com/pod-product-compliance
Lightning Source LLC
LaVergne TN
LVHW050339160826
845677LV00014B/3697

* 9 7 9 8 8 0 1 9 2 2 0 3 4 *